Praise for O ʟ̦ʏ

"Lawrence Edwards is that rare miracle—an authentic mystical poet inspired by direct experience of the divine. In *O My Beloved*, he offers us a gorgeous, wild, passionate, sacred feast. Eat, be inspired, rejoice, and keep using these messages from reality to embolden and ennoble your life."

—**Andrew Harvey**, author of *Turn Me to Gold: 108 Translations of Kabir* www.andrewharvey.net

"The jewels in this collection are translucent. By getting out of their own way, these poems let the divine light come streaming through."

—**Mirabai Starr**, author of *Wild Mercy: Living the Fierce and Tender Wisdom of Women Mystics* www.mirabaistarr.com

"These whisperings from the Divine are magnificent. As I read *O my Beloved*, I see spiritual seekers getting off their cushions, spreading out their arms to the sky, and breaking out in joyous song for the Divine Love thathas given them life. As the seekers find each other in dance, the surrounding clouds of doubt, fear, brokenheartedness, loneliness, and self-reproach fall away, revealing their fellow dancers, Buddha, Jesus, Lord Yama, Saraswati Devi, Mother Mary, Shekhinah, and Tara. Reading these poems is a *Lectio Divina*, changing us as we drink the nourishment of Kalidas' shared freedom."

—**Robert A. Jonas**, EdD, retreat leader, musician (*shakuhachi*), and founder and director of The Empty Bell sanctuary www.emptybell.org

"I love these poems! In his inspired *O My Beloved*, Lawrence Edwards put words to the timeless longing our soul feels for its source. Each poem has a power to pull the receptive reader into a deep meditative state filled with a love of the Divine. In this collection we find the extraordinary power of the fifteenth century devotional dialogue tradition effortlessly voiced in the twenty-first century. Moving and inspiring. Good company for anyone with a heart full of longing."

—**Lee Lyon**, founder and director of Foundation for Integrative Meditation, Santa Fe, NM, author of *The 112 Meditations from the Book of Divine Wisdom* www.integrativemeditation.org/about-lee-lyon

"When the Goddess speaks, she expresses the inexpressible. And this is exactly what she does when she speaks to the poet Lawrence Edwards. She expresses the inexpressible and then urges him, cajoles him, and spurs him on to find a way, to find the words that expresses it to the rest of us—to express the utter, unimaginable grandeur and glory of the Oneness of the All."

—**Teri Degler**, author of *The Divine Feminine Fire: Creativity and Your Yearning to Express Your Self* and *The Fiery Muse: Creativity and the Spiritual Quest* http://www.teridegler.com

"In his deeply felt book of spiritual poetry, Lawrence Edwards ascribes the beauty of his words with heartfelt modesty to the Kundalini goddess, Kali Ma, saying she chose him as a scribe to communicate her divine inspiration. We sense the unity of their connection in each line and observe the transcendent joy Edwards experiences in letting go of the all-too-human doubts and uncertainties produced by the mortal mind. This book is a celebration of his deep compassion for all that is known and unknown in our lives and for what is waiting for us when we shed our illusions, recognize that All is One, and embrace the universal love offered by Mahadevi in all her forms. No matter the source of the words, Edwards conveys his euphoric poetry with graciousness and passion, and each line is offered to us as a gift waiting to be unwrapped and savored."

—**Bruce Singer**, PsyD, clinical psychologist, mindfulness meditation teacher, musician, composer, and author of *Black Duck Moments Every Day* www.drbrucesinger.com

"Kalidas' renderings of these 'Whisperings' throb with the Divine presence. Evoking tears of longing and holy laughter, I found myself savoring them with long pauses to drink in the Beloved's blessings. The poems overflow with tenderness, passion for the Holy and compassion for the 'dear mind' that attempts to reign. Kalidas transmits the Devi's invitation to go—or be taken 'where mysteries beyond mysteries unfold.' Take Her up on her offer and 'hurl yourself in!'"

—**Sister Elizabeth Broyles**, CMA, cofounder, Companions of Mary the Apostle https://companionsofmarytheapostle.org/

"Passion, love, deity, dignity all clearly expressed in poetry rarely seen in today's creativity. Dr. Edwards reveals and revels in the deepest part of his Soul, welcoming our Souls to new heights and possibilities. His transparent love for the Divine, his passion, pours out with the dignity that only a worshiper of his caliber can express. Reading his new poetry took us to a level rarely acknowledged in our present day. What an experience!"

—**Charles Whitfield**, MD and Barbara Whitfield, CMT, RT, authors of *Healing The Child Within and The Natural Soul*, and other books www.barbara-whitfield.com

"In *O My Beloved*, Lawrence Edwards shares a precious song of devotion. These poems reflect both longtime spiritual practice and the immediacy and intimacy of moment that is the timeless center of that practice. In sacred and beautiful conversation, Edwards points toward a hopeful space where the longing and loving, broken and whole heart is unconditionally held."

—**Rachel Blum**, poet, author of *Doctor of Flowers* https://rachelblumpoetry.com/

"*O My Beloved* is an enchanting, mystical song of the Divine, leading the way to victory beyond the battlefields of life and death itself. Kalidas strikes with a clean sword, penning words that cut straight into the Heart of the One. What pours forth in these poems is Divinity's pure nectar. Each word, a vibration of the Divine, releasing and transmitting the purest of Love, bestowing grace and delight on every page. Kalidas guides us through a portal to a liberating journey from the finite to the infinite. A magical, masterful ride into the highest realms of the mystics, Gods, Goddesses, and into the abode of the One. Elevated into states of higher consciousness, this is our opportunity to take refuge and find the place of Union inside our own sacred, loving heart."

—**Anita Craig**, founder and director, FLOW, Future Leaders of the World (Pty) South Africa; and founding member of the Ganga Bhavani Maa World Trust https://www.futureleadership.co.za/

"The poems of Kalidas invite us to step outside our daily concerns and melt into the divine embrace. These songs remind us of our own inner voice in continuous, passionate dialog with the Divine Beloved. The language is often simple and direct, the honest, unadorned voice of the heart discovering new ways to surrender and open. A book to keep at arm's reach on the nightstand or near the altar."

—**Ivan Granger,** founder and editor of *Poetry Chaikhana*, author of *Real Thirst: Poetry of the Spiritual Journey*, and editor of *This Dance of Bliss: Ecstatic Poetry from Around the World* www.poetry-chaikhana.com

O My Beloved

WHISPERINGS FROM THE DIVINE

HEARD BY KALIDAS

Lawrence Edwards, PhD

Illustrations by Molly Edwards
Book design by Jess LaGreca, Mayfly Design
Cover image Tara thangka courtesy of exoticindiaart.com

ISBN (paperback): 978-0-578-37228-0
ISBN (ebook): 978-0-578-37229-7
Library of Congress Catalog Number: 2022902787

TSJ Publications
P.O. Box 87
Bedford, NY 10506
www.thesoulsjourney.com

Contents

Foreword

To read these poems is to enter holy ground, the sacred precincts of those who have read, thought, and lived sacred truth throughout a lifetime of dedication and practice. The speaker here is that rarity, a wise man in an age of triviality, a calm voice in a time of confusion. Lawrence has indeed been a lifetime seeker, and in these poems we are given the distillation of that search as he "brings the gift back home" (Joseph Campbell). Each poem reflects a sacred truth that we are reminded of with gratitude. Terms that may have seemed obscure are suddenly clear, old truths reaffirmed, and new perspectives revealed. As we move deeper into the collection, the verses more and more resemble the tone and texture of the ancient prophets, and we are reminded of those eras when truth speakers were not shy and listeners offered respectful attention.

Lawrence's basic message is the affirmation of Love as the essential necessity, and the Oneness of All as the ultimate realization. We are indeed fortunate to receive the wisdom here presented. Lawrence has invited us into his own prayer chamber, and there we are allowed not merely to witness but to participate in his own journey into transcendence. Savor each poem as a precious offering, a treasure to be prized. His language is replete with images and concepts drawn from his own long immersion in both Buddhist and Kashmiri Shaivite traditions. We are now the beneficiaries of his journey. Read them and find that your own journey is thereby enriched and abetted. Thank you, Lawrence, for this remarkable gift you have brought to us.

—Dorothy Walters, PhD
Dr. Walters is a poet and author of
The Goddess Speaks: Poems of Ecstasy and Transfiguration;
Kundalini Wonder: The god/goddess in Your Body,
and other books of poetry
http://kundalinisplendor.blogspot.com/

Preface

Please know, I'm not a poet! At best I'm a scribe, and a poor one at that! These writings are my effort as a scribe to put into words the gifts which Maa (Mahadevi, the Great Goddess, the Divine Mother) has metaphorically whispered or, at times, shouted in my ear!

My Beloved, known by so many names, though Kali and Tara are forms She frequently wears when visiting me, also delights in Being naked Awareness, pure Presence, Shiva—the Auspicious One, about which no one can ever truly speak or write. She is the source of these poems and writings, just as She is the source of the earlier collection, *Kali's Bazaar, Penned by Kalidas.* These are Her treasures that one of Her servants offers to you. Remember: Giver, Receiver, Gifts—all One, always, all One.

Some of Her gifts are wisdom instructions, some flow straight from Her all-embracing heart of Love, and others are incantations or proclamations of the Truth! "All is One! Shivo'ham!" resounds throughout the universe! Shivo'ham is an ancient Sanskrit mantra throbbing with the consciousness of "I Am the Auspicious One." The experience of that in the moment is one of the pure Awareness of that Reality, the whole universe, all space, all galaxies, all of creation down to the tiniest filaments of energy, throbbing with the Awareness of All is One, Shivo'ham. No words there, just unimaginably vast Awareness encompassing all, Being All, rapturously, ecstatically Being. The words came later as the poor little mind attempts to point to the infinite expanse of Reality with such pathetically limited symbols as words—words desperately trying to point beyond themselves to the Truth they can barely hint at. They are like a little sign a child may plant in their back yard, pointing up at the sky, saying, "Pluto—that way." The words are hinting at qualities of boundless Awareness that are *your very nature.* Go beyond the words to their Source!

Others of Her gifts invoke contemplation, blessings, Zen-like clarity, but most of all Love. Her call to freedom is Love. Her Love melts all boundaries, all pain, all separation, all . . .

May you receive the fullness of grace that She offers in every moment.

"There's never a time,
there's never a place,
that you're not in
the Divine's embrace!"
May you know that fully
with every thought in your mind
and every cell in your body.
May that direct knowledge inspire all your actions.
May we serve all with love, compassion and joy.

In Love and Service,
Lawrence

You Love The Masks

My friend,
You love the masks
But have yet to see
the faceless one.

You love the celestial choirs
But have yet to dissolve
in divine silence.

You love the dance of light and shadow,
the wind driven clouds,
But have yet to know the
Absolute stillness of resting
in the Beloved's embrace.

Come, She will show you the way
beyond the way.

Do You Know My Beloved?

Her fabric of life, so finely woven . . .
Threads of Herself made into cloth . . .
What's this thread to do
But quiver in Love.

She Drew Me Into

She drew me into
    Her womb,
all time and space,
innumerable universes,
infinite beings,
all held in Her
as Her.
Yet,
all,
all this,
the enormity of it all—
annihilating self—
all this
is but a speck
within Her!

Seek this with an adoring heart
only if you want to
cease to exist
as you.

All Is One

All is One
Shivo'ham!
All is One
Shivo'ham!*

Poor mind,
caught in constant
becoming,
desperately clinging
to a fictional me,
moment by moment
jumping so quickly
to identify
with a thought,
a feeling,
an action
in pursuit of likes
and avoidance
of dislikes.
So utterly exhausting
is this drama,
that by the end of the day
you collapse,
exhausted,
only to fall unconscious.

In that stillness,
in that silence,
you draw closer to the Truth
of who you are

than you ever get
while in your waking state.

Doing and becoming,
running toward,
running away,
you swing through time
bound to a pendulum
as much a fiction
as you.

Freedom literally requires
your undoing,
simply being
in utter stillness
utter silence.

Identify with anything
—instant bondage.

How to know
you are nothing
you are everything
you are both
you are neither
all simultaneously?

Dear mind,
this is beyond you.
The boundless grace
of true knowing,
illumined by the

Radiant One
whose Light
is pure Love,
happens in
the total stillness
and silence
of sweet union
with the Divine.

In that state
there aren't two,
not even one.
Dissolve in the
Divine embrace
for which there are
no thoughts or words.
Merge in the One,
the way of Love,
the only way of
true knowing.

*Ancient mantra: "I Am The Auspicious One"

If We Linger, Remembering

If we linger, remembering,
savoring
remembering,
savoring
the reminder,
a sound perhaps,
or two,
Om,
So'ham
will do,
or Lalla,
Kabir, Hafiz,
Mirabai . . . .
Is not the One
delighting equally
in the forgetting,
the reminder,
and the remembering?

So Much Doing

The yogis doing their pranayama,
Closing one nostril
Then the other.
Doing asanas
Doing mudras
Doing, doing, doing . . .

God waits

In the stillness
Of non-doing

In the deep stillness
Of utter abandonment

God breathing,
Breathing you
Into existence

God breathing
your in-breath

God breathing
your out-breath

God breathing
your in-breath

God breathing
your out-breath

Readying you
Steadying you

Ahhh, your
Final release
As your breath
Goes out,
Extinguishing the last
Flickering of
You,
As existence merges
In God.

What If?

What if you took birth
   to know radical freedom
Instead of constantly chaffing
   against the bonds of limitations.

What if you took birth
   to know radical freedom
from self-centered wants and needs,
To be carried by cascades of love
   along a river of ecstasy
with nothing to do but
   shout to the starving masses
      standing on the river banks
"Jump! Jump in! Jump in!
   You can be free of suffering!"

What if you took birth
   to know radical freedom and boundless love
instead of wandering lost in the torturous
   arid desert-maze of anger and fear.

What if you took birth
   to know radical freedom
Empowered to unfailingly choose
   the Way of compassion,
      wisdom and Love.

What if you took birth
   to know radical freedom

As taught by one fully awake -
    a buddha,
One who has gone beyond -
    a tathagata,
The Christ
    who taught the Way—
Do unto others as you would have them
    do unto you,
Who taught the sutras of selflessness,
    compassion, kindness and boundless, joyous Love
awakening you to why you took birth—
To rejoice every moment
    in the sea of agapé
To selflessly serve
    buoyed by the uplifting currents
        in the ocean of delight!

Having left behind
    the conditioned mind
Knowing radical freedom
You are the Buddha
You are the Christ
Gaté, gaté, paragaté, parasamgaté, bodhi swaha!*

*Sanskrit mantra from the Buddhist Heart Sutra
that means "Gone, gone, gone beyond, fully beyond, hail the goer,
so mote it be!"

11

She Visited Today

As I sat in the
Sweet stillness
Of simple emptiness
God stopped by.

She sat next to me
and asked,
"Anything you
need to know?"

I thought,
Okay, be bold!

So I asked
My Beloved,
how do you
see us?
So much is
written
about how we
see you.
More importantly,
how do you
see us?

As she looked at me
tears of love welled up
in Her eyes.
I wonder how long
She's been waiting
for that question!

She said,
O My Beloved,
You are my very
Self
asking your
Self
how your beloved
Self
sees Her Self!

See through
the eyes
of Love.
All will be clear.

The Pages Of Your Life

Though the pages of your life turn
one day at a time,
one breath at a time,
the book of your life is written,
And it is the book of love.
Love fills every page,
every breath.
All there is,
is love.

There's A Fragile Truce

There's a fragile truce
between stillness
and pain.
Stillness,
spacious and free,
invited pain to be at ease.
Pain,
unopposed,
receded back to its place
of ghostly potential.

Mind and body
take refuge in stillness,
spacious and free.

A Grateful Heart

O my Beloved,
I awoke today
buoyed by ocean swells of gratitude
for your countless gifts and
your sublime grace,
which you bestow
with such wild abandon!
Your inexhaustible generosity
humbles all who know you.

My Beloved,
I'm grateful for this human form
You created and endowed
with a mind, heart, and five senses
by which we delight in
your living Presence dancing
the dance of creation.

My Beloved,
I am ever grateful for this
loving heart of compassion,
your heart now beats in my chest.

My most treasured gift, my dearest,
is the deep knowing,
suffused with such indescribable adoration,
that reveals your graceful Presence
in every moment, every being,
and every atom of existence.
Surely you knew I would die

if ignorance ever separated me
from you again.

My Beloved Tara Ma,
at times I weep in rapture brought on
by your numinous, all-embracing Consciousness
flowing through this heart and mind,
body and soul,
now your heart, mind, body and soul,
feeling your seeking, ever seeking,
to relieve the suffering of all beings
throughout the universe.
Your loving compassion heals
all pain and sorrow.
May everyone find refuge in you.

My Beloved Devi,
who can express the overwhelming
gratitude that arises while seeing
you take every form needed to nourish
all beings, in all times and all places.
You've become the earth
to give us a home and shelter.
You've become food
to satisfy our hunger.
You've become drink
to slake our thirst.
You've become friends, family
and loved ones to support and guide us.
You've become strangers and enemies
to challenge us to expand our hearts.
O my Beloved, what won't you become

to ease our way home to you!
Grant me the clarity of mind and purity of heart
to fully appreciate all you become out of pure
love for every creature in your creation.

My dearest Beloved,
Time will never diminish my gratitude
for your revelation
that nothing exists outside
your loving field of Consciousness.
Within that boundless expanse
everything,
from galaxies to fleeting thoughts,
arises and subsides.
No mind can know the glorious mystery
of your loving power expressing itself by
creating all, sustaining all,
and dissolving all,
while never breaking your
sweet union with all.

By your gift of grace we awaken,
the illusion of separation dissolves,
and with it the ordinary mind.
All that remains is loving You,
beholding you as our own sublime Self,
the Self of all,
the Divine within all,
everywhere
the One,
whose nature is pure all-inclusive Love.
Nothing could ever exist outside of your
Divine embrace.

You want everyone to know
the unbreakable union
that brings an end to all suffering.

Seeker,
Live true to your boundless
loving nature,
for your nature is Her nature.
Om Tare Tam Soha.

Leave Behind The Ordinary Mind

(Hamsa is an ancient Sanskrit mantra meaning
"I Am That"—the All, the One)

Leave behind the ordinary mind!
Take refuge in the Truth!

All is One, I am that!
All One,
Hamsa,
All One,
Hamsa.

Upon waking,
All One,
Hamsa.

While sitting,
All One
Hamsa.

While walking,
All One,
Hamsa.

While standing,
All One,
Hamsa.

While gazing at the horizon,
All One,
Hamsa.

While sipping wine,
All One,
Hamsa.

In the company of others,
All One,
Hamsa.

While falling asleep,
All One,
Hamsa.

All One,
Hamsa,
All Love,
Hamsa,
All Love,
Tat twam asi!*

*Ancient Vedic mantra: "Thou Art That"

There's Never A Time

There's never a time,
There's never a place,
That you're not in
The Divine's embrace!

Awaken to this truth
And you will see
In the heart of God
You're always free.

Creator and creation
Eternally One
Pretending to be two
Just for fun!

Step out of the play
When you've had enough
In this illusory drama
Ignorance is painfully rough.

Take refuge in wisdom
Truly knowing Sofia's grace
Now look in a mirror
And see God's face.

Sweet Melody

The song of songs,
Sweet Melody,
Found me this morning
Dissolving me in her embrace.

Her throbbing pulse
Rippling out as all creation,
The carrier wave of Being, Consciousness, Loving Bliss . . .
Continuously birthing light and darkness,
Forms dancing in spacious emptiness.

Infinite vibrations—each a universe,
All throbbing as Her
As you
As me
All in all
Songs within songs within songs . . .

Sweet Gita,
Your Living Presence,
Delighting in simply being,
Being every living form.
Living galaxies,
Living rocks,
Living waters,
Living spirits,
Living creatures,
Living, throbbing, pulsing, singing,
Singing the eternal song of Being
Becoming,

Loving,
Dissolving,
Birthing it all,
Through ecstasy and pain,
Through the wild rapturous movement only
    an exploding star can express and
Through unfathomable, all-enveloping stillness.

She, we, hold all that in a small corner
of our vastness . . .
Time dissolves . . .

Our song continues,
Harmonies and dissonances
Arising from our one Being.
The pulse of our heart,
The rhythm of our breath
Emerging from sweet Melody,
Today,
Tomorrow,
For all eternity.

Shiva The Ravisher!

This morning all was erased—
Shiva the Ravisher
has bestowed his grace!
No one left but Shiva, Shiva, Shiva!
Body and mind wailing in tears of rapture,
pure ecstasy—everywhere Light, Love,
Shiva, Shiva . . . *

Shiva Shiva Mahadeva
Namah Shivaya Sadashiva!
All Shiva!
All Shiva!
All Shiva!

If you see any other
You are blind.

All Shiva!
All Shiva!
All Shiva!

If you see any other
You are lost in a dream!

Wake up!
Wake up!
It's all Shiva!
All Shiva!
All Shiva!
Namah Shivaya Sadashiva!

Shivo'ham!
Shivo'ham!
Shivo'ham!
Beat the drum of Shivo'ham!

*Ancient Sanskrit mantras:
Shiva (The Auspicious One)
Mahadeva (The Great Lord)
Shivo'ham (I Am Shiva)
Namah (I bow to)
Sadashiva (Eternally Auspicious)

And The One Spoke

And the One Spoke,
Saying:
If you want to know
Who you are,
I will show you
Who I truly am.

Behold earth,
The ground of your existence.

I became earth.
All elements and forms
I am.

Behold water,
Life's blood.

I became water.
All that flows
I am.

Behold fire,
Living flame of all life.

I became fire,
Dancing, illuminating, warming, transmuting.
Light and Life
Of the universe
I am.

Behold air,
Uplifting, carrying, dispersing.

I became air, wind, and storm.
Breath of life,
I am.

Behold space,
Embracing and penetrating
Atoms to galaxies.

I became space
Tenderly holding all my creation,

Nothing and no one is ever
left out.

Boundless heart of Love,
infinitely spacious,
I am.

Behold mind,
A ray of my Consciousness.

I became mind
Continuously moving,
Seeking
To know, to taste, to smell, to touch, to hear, to see
All I've become.
Sole Knower
I am.

Behold emptiness,
The magnificent black void.

I became emptiness,
Womb and tomb,
Bindu,
Portal between the
Finite and the Infinite,
Between the ephemeral
And the Eternal.
Cause of all causes
I am.

Behold pure Being
About which
Nothing can be said,
Not even by me.

Pass through the portal
And revel in knowing
You
are the One.

Arising In The Predawn Hours

Arising in the predawn hours
I go in silence to sit—
the meditation garden, flowers, bushes,
    Buddha—
all in stillness.

Dewdrops silently appear
    on Buddha's face,
like tears they run down his cheeks
      never disturbing his calm countenance.

Avalokiteshwara—the Eternal One
    forever shedding tears of compassion,
while sitting in utter stillness and silence,
      the flower and fruit of the Eternal One
      here and now.

Suffering ceases in knowing
    there is no other—
      only One,
      only One,
      only One.

Gaté paragaté parasamgaté bodhi swaha!

As The Giver

As the giver of all forms
        You are Mother.

As the dissolver of all forms
        You are my Lover.

O my Kali, my Beloved, my Self!
Love cures the pain of separation.

Om Kali Ma!
Om Kali Ma!
Om Kali Ma!

All This

All this
Only One
All this
Only One
All this
Only God
All this
Only One
All this
Nothing left out
All this
Only One
All this
All God
All this
All God
All this
All Love
All this
All Love
All this
Only you
All this
All you
All this
All Love
All this
Only God

All this
Only One
All this
Only One

(The universe resounds with this Awareness, beyond words, vibrating as Om)

Seeking The Master

Unknowing,
(how could they really),
they make their way
to the final refuge,
unaware of what their
soul endured
to have this precious encounter,
to see this knower,
karmic paths
entangled,
ancient mysterious
vines at last bearing fruit,
facets of Presence
reflected in
dew drops.

All meet only
themselves.
Projections,
longing,
hopes and fantasies,
disappointments,
worse—fulfillment.
Pleasures, spiritual
honey traps,
beckon.

So hard to know
there is no other.

Then, stripped naked,
clothes come off easily,
skin, muscle, and bones
part more reluctantly,
illusions find nothing
left to cling to.

Om purnamidah
Purnamidam . . .

The "me" they seek,
the "me" they think
themselves to be,
or not . . .
this enthralling play
of light and shadow,
Love Eternal,
in wild rapture,
delighting in becoming
every atom of
the Ephemeral.

To meet the One
be willing
to die
to all you know,
all you thought possible,
all you thought impossible.

What's left
just might serve
the way of Love.

My Beloved Tara Said

My Beloved Tara said:
Be awake and skillful
    in the present
And your past will reflect this.

Be awake and skillful
    in the present
And your future will be free of fear.

Be awake and skillful
    in the present
For only in this moment can your boundless
    Love, Compassion and Wisdom
Enter the world.

Bow Deeply

O mind,
bow deeply.
In so doing
you elevate
heart above head,
Love over all.
Know that you exist
to serve Love.
Know the sweet joy and
the fullness of gratitude
that wells up
as you fulfill
your sublime calling,
generously serving
all with Love.

They Didn't Set Out

When Buddha awoke to the highest Truth
he wasn't a Buddhist
He was Buddha.
He didn't set out to found a religion.

When Jesus knew "I and my Father are one,"
He wasn't a Christian
He was Christ.
He didn't set out to found a religion.

They've invited you to be a true knower.
Instead you've bound yourself
with ropes of orthodoxy and piety.
This is what you do with free choice?

So easy to become
A Christian, a Buddhist,
A Jew, a Muslim,
A this or that!

To know you are empty,
Nothing,
Is to be filled with the Light
Of true knowing
Of true freedom
Of true Love.
Come home to that.
You were born from that.
You are sustained by that.
You are that now.

All Shiva!

All Shiva!
All Shakti!
All Shiva!
All Shakti!
The play of two
        for the delight of One!
All Shiva!
All Shakti!
All you!
All me!
All Shiva!
All Shakti!
Hamsa!
Hamsa!
Hamsa!
Chidananda rupaha*
Shivo'ham, Shivo'ham!

*Sanskrit mantra: "I Am Consciousness and Bliss"

The Fire Of Kali's Love

My beloved Kali
sheds even her name,
like a negligee,
as we melt into
each other's
passionate embrace!

Nothing dare remain
near us
and risk being
set ablaze!

Even time knew
it had to disappear!
The distant forest
saw the dancing light,
yearning for a
spark of release,
the caress of
flames dancing
on wood . . .

Who is willing
to be consumed
in Her fire?

I Long To Know The Fullness Of Your Presence

My Beloved,
I long to know the fullness of your Presence,
cure my blindness,
let me see your infinite radiance
and witness your glorious effulgence!

Set free my heart
that it may drown in
your Love.

Time is precious.
Who but you knows
how long I have to live,
but how can I continue in this
world of darkness
without your living Presence?

My sweet Beloved answered:

My dear One,
remember what happened to Arjuna
when he asked for such revelations!

You live exactly as I want you to live.

How could it be otherwise?

The mind longs for dazzling clouds of Light
and miracles of cosmic Love.

I want you to know
my living Presence
has always surrounded you,
embraced you, engulfed you.
I gave you a body, mind and five senses
to delight in my company.
Each is a gateway to knowing Me.

I am the air breathing life
into you.
I am the earth supporting your every step.
Every morsel of food passing your lips is Me.
When water quenches your thirst,
it is I.
There's nothing you can touch or be touched by
that isn't Me.
I am all Light illuminating the darkness.
And, I am the darkness, the stillness, the silence,
inviting you to leave behind your fears
to pass through the portal to the eternal.

Every love, every joy
you have ever known
is Me,
and every sorrow and every pain.

I am all that is or ever will be.
I am you
discovering the ecstasy of becoming all,
while your pure boundless nature
remains untouched.

Know this
and truly see
truly be
awash in Love,
our true Presence.

If You Want To Follow

If you want to follow
The Way of Christ
open your heart
and simply Love.

Love every moment,
Love every creature,
Love every being,
Love yourself.
Love.

Pure Love
Unconditional Love
The Way of agapé
The Way of Jesus
The Way of radical freedom!

Free to Love all
In every moment,
Free to Love
At all times
In all places.

Free to be who you truly are—
Love,
Bringing the fullness of who you are
To all you encounter.

The boundless Love
Is the living presence of Jesus.

Following Love
Is following Jesus.

If you want to follow
The Way of Buddha
The Way of Compassion, Kindness
Patience and Love,
Know your Buddha nature,
Be true to your Buddha nature.
Offer that to every being
To all of creation.

Offer your Buddha nature—
Boundlessly kind
Boundlessly loving
Boundlessly patient
Boundlessly compassionate
Boundlessly wise
Eternally free!
Offer your Buddha nature
To all you encounter.

Following the Way of Buddha
Is not about simply sitting
Trying to be mindful.
It's offering the selfless
Loving compassion
You bring to each moment
To every being
To all of creation.

Most see two.
I only see One.

In The Temple

O my Beloved,
Here we are,
In the sacred predawn stillness,
Shrouded in silence,
Shrouded in darkness,
Like you my Beloved,
Shrouded in mystery!

Countless centuries,
Preparing the wick,
Lighting the oil lamp,
Your radiant presence
Illumines the temple.

This moment,
Outside of time,
Just the Eternal
Lover and Beloved,
Worshiper and worshipped.
Who is the wick?
Who is the flame?

It Started As A Practice

It started as a practice
so many decades ago
waking each day
to give thanks.

Imperceptibly, over time, Gratitude
softened my heart and
cleared my vision,
allowing me to receive
the extraordinary gifts
bestowed by the humble
presence of Gratitude.

She brought her companions,
Fullness, Abundance, and Generosity,
who always invite Delight to join them!

In their radiant company
Gratitude grew into
profound Appreciation for the
Living Presence of God
in every moment, every being, everything,
filling heart and soul with Love,
wellspring of the Eternal One.

May Gratitude and her companions
illumine your heart
every day of your life!

Keep The Light Of Love

Keep the light of Love
before you, my dear.
See all illuminated by Love.
The ever-present
Lord of Love, infinitely radiant,
bathes you and all you perceive
with Love.

You are a ray of that Love.
Give up pretending
to be anything else!

Reveal your true nature
to yourself and the world!
Your loving presence
is so desperately needed now.

Look Around

Look around
        what do you see?
Only the Beloved!
Only the Beloved!
All or nothing!
All or nothing!
Only me!
Only me!
Everywhere, look!
Only mirrors
Only mirrors
Nothing else to see
Let go and let go . . .
Simply BE
Simply BE
Bare and Free
Truly see!
Aham Brahmasmi!*

*Ancient Vedic mantra: "I Am The Absolute."

49

This Pitiful

This pitiful
puny puddle
barely filled,
constantly emptied
by the five waters,
dries up in no time.

What ignorance,
what arrogance
drives you
to proclaim
your ephemeral
pitiful, puny puddle
to be better,
more deserving
than any other?

The great equalizer,
Lord Yama,   (Lord of Death)
has your number!
He's at your shoulder
right now!
Can't you hear
his soft laugh?

Only one way through.
Beat Death to death!
Die once and for all!
Die into the Eternal!
Die into God!

The Veil Of Ignorance

The veil of ignorance
gives birth to fear.
Fear, seeking relief,
clings desperately to some forms,
runs from others,
careening through ghostly forests
of its own imagining.

Lifetime after lifetime
searching desert mirages
for She who flows,
but can never be found
by fear driven ones.

O Saraswati Devi!*
Send your life-giving waters,
streams of mantra,
to rescue all who are
wandering, lost
in this desert
of ignorance.

*Saraswati is the ancient Great Goddess whose name means "she who flows."

You're Such A Sieve!

O mind,
You're such a sieve!
That's the nature
the Divine gave you!
Give up trying
to hold
and let yourself
be held!
The blissful ocean
of Love,
the Infinite One,
Awaits!
Hurl yourself in!

Vaulted Cliffs

Vaulted cliffs
   and towering pines,
Nature, my cathedral,
   welcomes me home.
Wandering streams, dancing waterfalls
   and clear serene lakes,
All-embracing wind and
   boundless sky . . . .
The living Presence
   of the Radiant One
Dispels the mists
   of unknowing,
All is One,
All is One,
All is One.

Jai Shiva Nataraj!*

Wild, wild dancer!
Locks flying
Swirling faster
faster, faster
Shakti flying off
like sparks in a gale
roaring through
a blazing forest,
Swirling and twirling
Tighter and faster
The still point
Beckoning ever more
Insistently,
Cries of ecstasy
Shatter time
Explode space
All forms released!
Cosmic nuclear fusion
Infinite Shakti exploding!
The still point opens!
The boundless spaciousness
Of pure Being,
No other,
No movement.
All is One!
All IS ONE!
Shivo'ham!
Shivo'ham!

*Lord of the Dance

My Beloved Brought Me To Her

My Beloved brought me to Her
midnight portal,
entryway to mysteries beyond mysteries.
I peered into the Infinite Dark,
Her formless Presence,
knowing the boundless Love
of ecstatic dissolution
She was drawing me into.
Fear and trepidation have long fled,
yet ecstatic trembling seizes this body!
O the blissful anticipation that is given
to mind and body, heart and soul!
Her luscious embrace pulls
what remains of a me
into the dark,
now, suddenly, radiant
with flames of Love blazing everywhere!
All is aflame!
All is alight with Her fire!

She is the Fire, the Love,
birthing infinite forms,
all within Herself,
all radiant with Her
Living Presence!
All forms are Her!
Only Her, dancing everywhere!
O my Beloved,
grant this vision to everyone!
How can we breathe without knowing
the Fire of Your Love?

My Beloved Kali

My Beloved Kali
standing before me
gracing me with your presence earlier today
I noticed a dim light in the sky
off in the distance
over your shoulder.

Suddenly I realized
it was the sun!
your magnificent darkness,
your mysteriously radiant blackness,
outshines
even the sun!

Were it not for your will
holding together the threads of energy,
your energy,
that makes the appearance
of this mind and body possible,
surely in this instant
they would ecstatically
dissolve back into their source,
making it clear to all
that you alone
exist.
There is no other
here.

O Weary Soul

My body's dead,
My memory's erased.
My Lord's name,
Is all I that's left, says Kabir.

O weary soul,
Take refuge in the name!
Shiva Shiva Mahadeva
Namah Shivaya!

Om Namah Shivaya!
O ocean of mercy!
O infinite expanse
Of all-embracing love!
O boundless sea of
rapturous ecstasy!

You bestow your grace
on those wandering in the
liminal grounds of
death and sacrifice.

Having nothing left
to lose
they are ripe
for your gift,
the ultimate disillusionment.
Now giver, gift and receiver
merge in the bindu of your Beloved!

Nothing remains
but the whispered throb
of your name—
Shiva
Shiva
Shiva

My Dear Sweet Soul

My dear sweet soul,
lifetimes of longing
lifetimes of searching,
grace has now brought you
into the arms
of the Beloved.

Rest in the Divine embrace!
Quiet the mind's agitation.
Silence is the language
of sublime Love.

Explanations, justifications,
confessions,
have no place
in the arms of the Beloved!

Be still!
You are completely loved
You are completely lovable.

In the stillness of pure Being
melt
melt the illusion of two
melt in quiet rapture
melt 'til all is Love,
eternal
inexhaustible
all-embracing
Love,
God's living presence.

The Living Flame Of Love

The living flame of Love
Igniting the root
Burns upward
Consuming the wick
Knot by knot.
Soften, melt.
Be drawn up into
The holy fire.
First the body
Incandescent with love
Sets the mind ablaze.
Freed from self,
Love's unbearable fire then feasts on the final knot,
The dark cause of all causes
Vanishes,
Vanquished by Love's boundless radiance.
The painful illusion of separation exploded.
No thing
No one
Remains.

Author's note: the wick symbolizes the sushumna nadi, the knots are the granthis, the causal body is the cause of all causes—ignorance of the Divine.

My Lord

My Lord,
Our God
spoke:
If you want
to be filled,
first you must
be emptied.
Completely.

Remain empty and
I will fill you.

Remain empty,
I will fill you.

Remain empty,
I will fill you
with Love
every moment
from now
through eternity.

No Matter

No matter how I refine the symbols,
or mold myths and metaphors,
the One lies beyond.

No matter the music, the chants and mantras, the drum beats,
the blowing of conches, and the resounding nada,
the One lies beyond.

No matter the statues, pictures, visions, yantras,
thangkas, icons, and scrolls,
the One lies beyond.

No matter the sublime touch, the ambrosial tastes,
the divine embrace, consolation gifts for all the senses,
the One lies beyond.

Leave it all,
Leave everything behind!
Enter the portal

•

Her bindu,
where mysteries beyond mysteries unfold.
Gone, gone, gone beyond . . . .

O My Beloved

O my Beloved,
calling your name
your sublime scent pulls me
into the dark passage
leading to your
secret abode.
This body disappears
   in the shroud of darkness.
This mind dissolves
   in the throb of *Kali, Kali, Kali*.
As the last wisp of me
   merges in She,
Darkness bursts into
   the Light of a million suns!
Unbearable Light—rapturous, ecstatic Light,
   'til none remain.
No one.
No other.
No thing.

Come Home Now

O dear mind,
you struggle
in your world
of self-created differences
trying to unite that
which was never divided.

O dear mind,
for you,
loving all and knowing all
are true mysteries
lost in the impenetrable darkness
of unknowing.

O dear mind,
your unknowing
is a consequence
of your very nature.

O dear mind,
you exist to know
differences, limitations,
the finite world
of your existence.

O dear mind,
you skillfully divide the Infinite
into tiny pieces
and suffer the loss
of your boundless
all-encompassing source.

O dear mind,
this is what is
symbolized by your
ouster from Eden
when you became aware of
the polarities, pairs of opposites,
good and evil being just one,
that appear to separate you
from your Divine source,
the Infinite,
from which you can never be
truly separated.

O dear mind,
you were created
to explore, know, and identify with
the components
of your perceptions,
the five empty skandhas
Buddha viewed while coursing through
deep prajna paramita.

O dear mind,
your way of knowing
is rooted in the illusion
of separateness
and independence.
Your way of knowing
is the source
of your suffering.

O dear mind,
see through the eye
of the Infinite One!
Knowing and Loving,
bound to the appearance
of separateness
by your language,
are *one* for the Divine.

O dear mind,
Knowing all *is* loving all.
Loving all *is* knowing all.
Loving all *is* knowing all are One.
All One
All One
All One
There is no other.
God, the One known by many names,
sees only One.

O dear mind,
the mystics of every tradition
come to know this same truth.
There is only One.
Tat twam asi!
Aham Brahmasmi!
Shivo'ham!
Ein od milvado.
St. John of the Cross said
when God looks at the world
all he sees is himself!

O dear mind,
the only way to know this
is to dissolve into the One.
Relinquish for a moment,
longer if you can,
this illusion of separation
that you cling to.
Don't worry,
you will return to your
job of seeing differences,
but your vision will be forever
transformed,
informed by deep knowing.

You are the Divine's own creation
for knowing separation and difference.
Even in the depths of ignorance,
even in the depths of suffering,
you are the Divine,
forever known and loved,
forever living in the Divine embrace.
Come home now
to knowing/loving all,
including yourself,
just as the One
created you.

Come home now
and know true freedom
from suffering.

Flawed

O my Beloved Tara!
Your pure magnificence,
your boundless, overwhelming,
self-annihilating infinitely Loving nature,
embracing all,
cradling all,
tenderly caressing all,
Your blessed touch
going unnoticed,
demanding no attention,
no self in need of recognition,
Your quiet perfection
reveals the way.

Tarama, bless this little one
that he may be
your flawed servant
'til all are free.

O Divine Mother

O Divine Mother
How have you given birth
To all this!
Now my Beloved,
Grant my wish
That everyone see
Through the veil,
Knowing your loving
Embrace, here, now
Forever!
Please my Beloved,
Remove all forms of suffering,
All causes of suffering,
Setting everyone free
To revel in Love,
Your palpable presence.
I died my last death
In your Love.
Give this freedom
To all beings,
My Beloved.

Om Kali Ma
Om Kali Ma
Om Kali Ma

Om Namah Shivaya

My beloved Shiva,
Your tender embrace
floods my eyes with tears,
now streaming down
onto your graceful feet.

These are the tears
of Mary washing
the feet of Jesus.

These are the tears
of Mirabai
longing for her Lord.

These are the tears
of your devotees
at the wailing wall.

These are the tears
that have streamed down my face
onto Bhagawan's blessed padukas,
onto my Baba's feet,
onto my beloved Kali's breasts,
onto my puja and robes.

What have I to offer
but tears, my Lord.

Early Morning

Early morning
     two owls wildly hooting,
spring moonlight dancing,
while only a few hours remain
     'til dawn silences these merry sages
          for whom darkness is light
               and light is darkness.
Their vision and voices
     pierce the night,
I laugh out loud
     in pure delight,
hoping of course
     that I do not wake
my sleeping wife!

Hooting and hooting while the moon looks on,
     the exuberant barred owls sing
          their duet like drunken friends beneath a street light!

O my mind,
why do you turn
     from joy to annoyed?
Are you so attached
     to sleep-laden unconsciousness
that even a rare pleasure
     visiting longer than desired
provokes agitation?

Let go, let go dear friend,
    part the curtains, throw open the
        window,
bathe in delight!'

You Think

You think God
      doesn't fill you
           moment by moment?

You think you do
      all the important
           things in your life?

You think you survive
      and even thrive
           by the strength of your will?

Good!
Now, exhale and use your great will
      to refuse the inhalation.

How long can you thwart
      the in-breath—the inspiration?
           Inspiritus! And so God enters her creation!

You will continue inspiration, expiration,
      inspiration, expiration . . . .
           until God stops breathing you
                  into existence one breath at a time.

God fills you
      with the breath of life
           and quietly whispers, O so softly,
                 the noisy mind never notices,
                     I AM with each breath.

The Divine Presence is irresistible! She is your living breath!

Here's the real secret—
       She loves you in ways you cannot begin to imagine,
         but become truly quiet and She'll draw you
             into the great stillness where all is revealed!

I, I, I, Me, Me, Me

I, I, I, me, me, me, mine, mine, mine.
Caught in the cocoon of limited self
the soul spins its reality
lifetime after lifetime,
clinging and clinging
to its little creation.

The One awaits
with loving arms
embracing the little one
lost in its dream.

The One sees
only itself . . .
the dreamer
the dream
the One
All One
Only One
Tat twam asi!

Jai Maa!

The Secret Cave

As a young man
I heard ancient tales of a secret cave
at the bottom of the ocean
where gold and jewels
beyond measure lie.
Inexplicably, such a longing
ignited within me
that I moved to the seashore.
Day after day,
I dove deeper and deeper
into the ocean.
Day after day,
I entered the inky blackness
where the light of the world
fails to reach.
At times I returned to the surface
covered in sea weed
looking like an alien creature.
After some years
people no longer recognized me.

Though unseen, I could feel the radiance
of the hidden treasure
as if it were in my heart,
drawing me ever deeper,
diving beyond sight and sound,
the pressure of the abyss
pounding in my ears.
At last, my fingertips
groping in the dark,

found an opening
to an underwater cavern
in the bedrock of the sea floor.

My lungs nearly burst
as I drew myself up a dark passage into the cavern,
which held sweet life-giving air.
Light shown everywhere,
blinding my eyes so accustomed
to the black void of the ocean depths!

Gold and jewels glowing like fiery embers
lay in mounds as far as I could see
in this underwater,
underground cathedral.
My heart leapt,
these treasures will remove
the suffering of countless people in need!
I took all I could carry
hoping to find my way back
to the surface
and back down again for more.

As I left the cave,
diving back into the black
water-filled tunnel and
swimming for the surface,
I was shocked to feel
the gold and jewels
crumbling, disintegrating,
as they slipped back
into the dark void

that is their home.
By the time I reached the shore
all my hands clutched
was a bit of shiny dust.

Collapsing on the beach I wept.
What have I to give away?
The true existence of that hidden,
radiant treasure called to me again and again.
Yet every time I returned to the secret cave
trying to bring even one gem back,
all that remained as I surfaced
was dust.

So I sit on the seashore babbling
to passersby
about hidden treasures in a secret cave
deep below the ocean waves.
I know the way there and back,
I tell them,
but what good is it they ask,
if you can't do anything with it.

I no longer need to dive into the ocean
to visit the secret cave.
The longing that awoke within me
so very long ago
grew into a blazing fire.
That light, just like the light in the cavern,
fills the cave of my heart with a warm radiance
suffused with love for all.

Ahhh, the fullness of Self-Luminous Being,
free from all wants and needs!
I'm awash with unspeakable joy!
Now that Light fills my vision!
All I see is that sublime Light
embracing all with Love!
One day we will enter the cave
never more to return.

Great Dark

The leaden Dark,
dulling, numbing, deathly darkness,
now is waning.
I've come to know your ways,
O great Dark.
You leave,
but never entirely.
Your sister
illumines you
even when your thick
black presence
covers all,
crushes all,
squeezes all life
love, joy and kindness
from the very bones of existence.

Even then O great Dark,
you are at her mercy.
I've seen you surrender to her
without a fight.
I know your dance now.
You can no longer frighten me.
I see how tenderly your sister
treats you, O great Dark.
And, I see how you simply melt
in her presence.

She is my Lady of Light,
my Beloved,
who ignited my soul
and accompanies me everywhere.
I see you retreating whenever we approach.
I'd invite you to play,
but you are powerless to draw near.
It is fun to chase you from enclosures that
only fear and ignorance can create.

M'lady says this play of light and shadow
has existed for all time.
I don't have her patience.
I would set the universe ablaze
to annihilate your darkness and
all the suffering you impose.
But even Buddha couldn't rid
the world of Mara.

Instead M'lady, set me free!
Darkness, O great Darkness,
We see through your illusions,
even your power is empty.
We invite all to know this and be free.

Your Gentle Breath

O my Beloved,
Your gentle breath upon my chest
    awakened me in the night.
Your warmth embraced
    flesh and bone,
        heart and soul,
Your breath
    breathing me
        'til only your breath
            remains.
The great swan
    takes flight,
Hamsa dissolves into
    Your boundless radiance
        where no other can go.

You Don't See Me!

My beloved,
You see what I've become
but you don't see me!
I'm delighted you're so enthralled
by all the forms my dancing
energy takes!
Earth, water, fire, air,
galaxies and universes!
Beings beyond number!
Countless minds and
all they think!
Life and death in all their
glory and gore!

Yes, I become all that is
Or ever will be.
But, my dearest, you don't see *me*.

You tire of knowing
what can be seen.
Now dissolve back into the
One who's never seen,
yet sees all.
It's the only way to know
me, my beloved,
and to know the infinite Love
that has become this
magnificent universe,
holding it all
in Love's sublime embrace.

Know me in the stillness
of complete surrender,
beyond seer and seen,
where our eternal union
alone exists.

What Will You Reflect?

O Mind,
Can you reflect
the unborn One?
Can you reflect
the undying One?

Covered in the
dung of ignorance,
countless stinging flies
plague you night and day!

"I can't stand this!"
"I hate that!"
"You're so irritating."
"I want more of this."
"I want to be rid of that."
"I need you to stay forever."
"I need you to go and never return."
"That puts me in bliss!"
"That makes me so angry."

O mind,
remove the layers of ignorance
by which you cling to unknowing.
The mirror isn't stained
by what it reflects.
Throw off the cloaks
of self-deception,
watch suffering depart.

Bathe in the truth
of pure Being
unborn
undying,
bathe in the truth,
HAMSA!

Witness lifetimes of ignorance
dissolve in the currents
of pure knowing,
freeing the mind of all afflictions.

Know the boundless equanimity,
joy, love and compassion
reflected in your purified form,
O mind!
Dissolve again and again
in stillness,
in silence,
beyond all thoughts and words.
Dissolve into the eternal
Presence of the One!

What Will You Become?

What will you become, my little one?

I don't seek oneness with Lord Krishna,
nor to be his devotee,
not Arjuna,
nor Yudhishthira,
not even a Gopi.
No, I've become his flute,
awaiting his warm hands,
his moist lips,
the thrill of his breath
awakening sounds of delight
carried by the winds throughout the world
that others may know
the throb of his heart,
his song of God,
His breath of Love.

I don't want to be the Master,
nor his disciples—
Simon, Peter,
John nor Matthew,
not Phillip nor James,
for I became the one
washing his feet
with my tears of love.
I am Mary, summoned by him
to see the Divine through the eyes of love,
to welcome his return from the dark womb
of the Mother.

He said, "be not afraid," and I wasn't.
He ignited the flame of the eternal within me.
Love exalted moves beyond time.
One heart,
One love,
the Kingdom of God spread upon the earth.
He told me to go, spread the good news,
Forever one in heart,
One in Love
Wherever I go there He is.

I hear all those who want to know
their Buddha nature.
I have no want to be a Buddha,
nor a Buddhist,
nor a tathagata,
not a bhikshuni or bhikshu.
I am filled with
Buddha's warmth
as he slips his feet
into me, his sandals,
and traverses the worlds,
radiant, illuminating the way.
I protect the Blessed One
as he walks the paths of eternity,
like dharma for those who walk the way
of wisdom and compassion.

I see the sweet lovers
of Kwan Yin
begging for her blessings,
or sitting in silence,

attempting to merge with her sublime nature,
to experience the boundless compassion
of the ineffable One.
I am what she wanted,
a simple pitcher,
a small vessel in her hands.
O, if you knew her touch you would never want more!
Never emptying,
She pours her inexhaustible
Love,
drawn from the wellspring of the eternal,
into the thirsty mouths
of all those suffering
throughout time.

What can I ever become
except what She chooses.

We, All Beings

We, all beings,
all creation,
are the unknowing
of God.

Unknowing
gives birth
to all things.
Unknowing is
ignorance,
except for the
Divine,
for which
it is merely
a self-imposed precondition
for knowing
unknowing!

The Infinite Divine
is infinitely
curious
and delights
in knowing
all possible
forms
of unknowing.
It alone
is the knower
and the known,
knowing and
unknowing.

The Moment You Were Born

The moment you were born
your death became certain.
As vigorously as the mind
denies its end
it denies the depths
and riches of its very existence.
Ephemeral distractions and pleasures
are impoverished substitutes.

Plumb the depths of death
and you'll find the
Mother of all!
O Mata Kali!
You reveal all
to those who take
refuge in you!
Setting your lovers
free from the fear of death,
You hold them in Your
eternal embrace!

Wandering Through The Forest

Wandering through the forest
we come upon an open glade.
O my Beloved,
suddenly You let the fullness
of your Divine Presence
be known,
enveloping,
no,
Being!
all I perceive!
You, the soft petal of the
late winter crocus,
You, the scent of ground
thawing, leaves decaying,
incense suffused with You
my Beloved!
Shafts of sunlight
amidst columns of trees,
You! You, my Beloved!
Daffodil shoots
and promises
of brilliant yellow blossoms,
You! You, all You!
Who's experiencing all this!
Perceiver and perceived,
mind and body,
You! You, all you!
Lover and Beloved,
You! You, only You!

Nothing left but You!
Om Kali Ma!
Om Kali Ma!
Om Kali Ma!

Pointless

You are the point
Or at least that's
What dominates
Your view.

Your point
may be huge,
O so grand,
Or at least that's
Your view.

Your point
may be tiny,
O so insignificant,
Or at least that's
Your view.

Your point
your I
your me
whatever its size
is your prison.

To be free
is to be free
of me.

How liberating!
Be pointless!

The Truth And The Way

The Truth and the Way
Eternally present
Here and now
Summoning you,
whispers of Love
on the wind,
do you hear?
Are you prepared
for revelation?
For rapture?
Turn toward the One,
surrender,
Grace will do
all that's necessary.
Turn toward the One,
gaze unwaveringly,
Creator and creation
merge.

Revelation?
How could the
Infinite Radiance
of the Divine
ever be hidden?

O mind,
you are the instrument
God created for
Self-forgetting!
For perceiving

the finite in the Infinite!
For imagining absence
where there is only Presence!
What a marvelous creature
you are!

As the veil of Self-forgetting
begins to thin,
after countless lifetimes,
the seed of knowing
the Truth and the Way,
lying dormant within you for eons,
begins breaking through
the hard shell of ignorance,
yearning for the Light,
longing for the boundless
radiance of the Infinite!
Your true Self,
Your true home.

Illumined by Grace,
the Divine's power
of revelation and transformation,
the Way begins to appear!
It happens in a manger,
under a bodhi tree,
in a village,
in a desert,
in a prison,
in a city,
in a forest,
any time,

any where
one is ripe for knowing.

Now mind,
you have a habit of
grasping, clinging,
proclaiming ownership
of what you like and want!
You do this as ego mind,
individually, and as group ego mind!
Watch what happens
as you do this!
The Truth is obscured,
The Way is distorted,
you heap layers of
complex practices,
dogma and orthodoxy
on the Light of the Divine,
confusing and prolonging
the suffering of countless
weary souls longing
to return home to
God's embrace.
Stop!
For your own sake,
for the sake of all beings,
Stop!

The Truth and the Way
Eternally present,
here and now,
summoning you,

whispers of Love
on the wind,
do you hear?
Are you prepared
for rapture?
Don't worry,
neither was Mary!

The Divine
created you to know
the ecstasy of return!
The torturous illusion of separation
dissolves into the One
rapturous embrace!
St. John of the Cross said
All God sees is Himself!
That's all there is!
Only One,
there is no other.
Every true knower of every sublime tradition
comes home to the same One!
Ein od milvado!
Aham Brahmasmi!
Om mani padme hum!
Shivo'ham!
All rivers merge in the ocean!

The Truth and the Way
are One.
Knowing and Loving
are one for the One.

You are completely known,
completely Loved.
The Truth and the Way
are all-embracing Love.
In every moment,
turn toward Love.
In all beings
see Love.

Love, boundless,
radiant, all-encompassing,
the Truth and the Way.
Tat twam asi!
Thou art That!

Now, serve all
in Love
with all!

Surprise, I'm Here!

Driving to my office,
not much to do.
Quiet pandemic times,
taking the back way,
a mom, dad and child,
walking hand-in-hand
their little one skipping and laughing
between them in the clear spring sun,
her face as bright as the daffodils along the roadside.
Suddenly tears of love
flood my eyes!
You're everywhere!
You're everyone!
You're everything!
The mom, dad and child,
each a universe of Love with
their own galaxies of creation
whirling within them!
Car, road, mind, body—
Love loving form!
Love lovingly becoming form!
Dharma, seva, work, practice,
All Love becoming, becoming, becoming . . .
You ambush us with Love!
You ambush me even as me!
Your ever-new
eternally fresh
revelations of your
Loving Presence,

You even create thin veils
for the delight of suddenly
dissolving them . . .
Surprise, I'm here!

The Infinite One

The Infinite One
　　lovingly watches
the ardent soul working
　　so painfully hard
to escape the dark prison cell
　　she has awakened in.

Longing to enter the Light
　　of the Infinite One,
whose radiance she caught
　　a glimpse of
through a tiny crack high
　　on the stone wall,
she struggles to be free.

Clawing at the stone
　　she has no idea
the One has dissolved all
　　but the last layer
separating Its dear soul
　　from her Source.

The stone strengthened
　　the soul's resolve.
As she breaks through the wall,
　　triumph and profound relief
suddenly give way
　　　　to laughter and delight!

It was all a play of the One!
No pain, no suffering, no separation
    were ever real!

If You Want The Truth

If you want the truth,
    here it is:
You have a mind, but it doesn't belong to you.
God created the mind as an instrument for Her creativity.
Give your mind back to God and experience the ecstatic symphony
    She plays through Her mind.
Give your mind back to God and see Her boundless love
    everywhere, embracing all.

If you want the truth,
    here it is:
You have a body, but it doesn't belong to you.
God created the body and its senses to enjoy Her creation.
Return your body to God and know Her boundless delight!

The Clever

The clever
see differences.
The wise
see unity.
The enlightened
merge seer and seen
beyond unity and diversity.

O Mata Kali

O Mata Kali,
black is your womb
birthing time and space,
mysteries beyond mysteries.

Incandescent is your blazing love,
flaming portal to freedom
beckoning all lovers
of the Divine!

Om Kali Ma!
Om Kali Ma!
Om Kali Ma!
Namo namaha.

Discard All

Discard all
but Essence.
Go within,
enter the stillness
beyond silence.
Die to all
that is other.
Die into Essence,
you will live
in God alone.

Better To Die

Better to die in remembrance of our oneness with God
     than to live in a desert of forgetfulness.
Better yet to live in oneness with God
     and go beyond death.

I Abandoned Myself

I abandoned myself
    to find God.
When I found God
    I found my Self.

God Said

God said:
I am
mantra.
The mind
is words,
My matrika shaktis.

The universe
Is mantra.
Truth resounds
as mantra.
Take refuge
in me.
Hamsa

If It Is Not Known

If it is not known
in the stillness,
in the absolute silence
of no-self,
then it is not known.

If it is not known
in the stillness,
in the absolute silence
of no-self,
it is not worth knowing.

Like The Countless Rays

Like the countless rays of the sun,
    one source, one essence,
So are we all
    emanations of the Divine One.

Little Mind

Little mind playing in its sandbox,
Mother calls,
Illusion shatters!

She Threw Me Out

She threw me out of her pleasure grove again.
It happens all the time, but I can't say I like it!
I know she'll take me in her arms again,
For now, my eyes can't help but see her
in you.

Why Speak To The Brush

Why speak to the brush
When the artist
Is right here?

Why speak to the pot
When the potter
Is right here?

Why speak to the scribe
When the author of it all
Is right here?

At First You Might

At first you might only
hear the flute's music.
Follow it to its source!
Lord Krishna awaits!

When I Found

When I found my heart
I found the Lord
When I found the Lord
I found my heart.

When God Said

When God said,
"O my beloved,
your eyes are the eyes of God,
your ears are the ears of God,
your face is the face of God,
your hands are the hands of God,
your whole body is the body of God,
God created your magnificent form
to know God as you,"
She meant it!

Snow Melts

Snow melts,
    cherry blossoms appear,
Now, crimson leaves
    and geese fill the sky.

The Chrysanthemums

The chrysanthemums died in the first winter snow.
Now they adorn the compost pile.
The empty clay pot
rests contented.

Window Washing

Washing the windows—
Is the dirt inside or out?
Ahhh, both need cleaning!

When The One

When the One
plays as two
limitless delight
soon ensues!

We Enter Silence

We enter silence not so much to pray to God,
but to hear God's prayer,
to feel His living Presence,
to be erased by Love.

You are the whispering of God
to God.

A Blessing

May you visit often
your heart of hearts
Where the wellspring of Love
nourishes all you care for.
May you discover the mysteries of how
Love's power sustains your life.
May the wellspring of Love
soften the ground of your life and
make it fertile.
May the Love emanating from your good heart
caress all who come near you.
You are born of love,
Your every breath arises
and subsides from the ocean of Love
we call God.
May you always know what God knows:
You are completely lovable
and you are completely loved.
You are held in the arms
of Divine Love,
Now and forever.

For The Love Of Light

For the Love of Light
We celebrate
The winter solstice,
The oil lamps remaining lit,
The baby born in a manger,
Buddha's enlightenment,
The luminous words of sages and saints
All pointing to the true Light,
Whose nature is all-embracing Love.
We celebrate
The One taking forms
To deliver us from the darkness
Of ignorance,
Illuminating the Way.
For the one true Way
Is the Light of Love.
Follow Her
And know the Divine embrace,
Know boundless, eternal Love.
Happy Holy Days To All!

New Year Blessing

May the New Year open its arms to you
as a lover too long separated from her beloved.

May the wondrous possibilities unfolding through time
bring your soul into communion with your Source.

May you know that what is past is truly gone, dissolved back into the
Great Mother, persisting only in the mind clinging to it.

May Ma Kali dissolve all that binds you as easily as she dissolves
every moment, every hour, every day, every year—disappearing
forever in her mysterious black void.

May wisdom infuse your heart and mind
with compassion, clarity, and patience.

May you see and feel the boundless love of the Divine
within everyone and everything at all times.

May the inexhaustible wellspring of your heart's loving kindness
flow through you unimpeded, nurturing all you encounter.

May this year bring you closer to fully realizing the hidden majesty
and glory illuminating the purpose of your life moment by moment.

May you peacefully walk the earth effortlessly radiating
the Light and Love that are your true nature.

New Year Contemplation

Beginnings require preparation, heightened awareness, and loving attention. The more significant the endeavor the more we must bring these fully into the moment.

As you begin, may you bring the full power of your heart, mind, body and spirit
   to the start of the New Year
   to this day
   to this hour
   to this moment!
   Right here, right now!

Remember that loving attention is the most valuable resource in the world. Without attention nothing flourishes. Without loving caring attention life withers and dies, relationships wither and die, even nature will wither and die.

What do you truly love?
What do you truly value?
What are you whole-heartedly committed to?
How much time and attention do you give each day to what you profess to value?

Globally, huge energies of transformation are stirring as people awaken to our interdependence with all people, creatures, plants—the entire web of life on our planet.

The old evolutionary paradigm of survival of the individual ensuring the survival of the species has collapsed.

We need to give our loving attention to the care of ALL.
There is no *us vs them*. Our evolutionary challenge now is to evolve to an all-inclusive WE.

WE can and will transform social and economic structures to serve the promotion of our loving care for ALL.

WE can and will act to disempower those who seek domination, exploitation and control for amassing obscene levels of wealth and power. Such people suffer a pathology that inflicts suffering on billions of people and countless living things. Why seek to emulate them or hold them up as examples of good leadership? The shadow side of the power drive in individuals, corporations, groups and nations needs to be illuminated, confronted, restrained and transformed.

In this moment, in this new beginning, commit your loving attention to your highest calling!

Bring your spiritual practices into every moment for the relief of suffering of ALL.

We are evolving peaceful warriors on a mission to bring loving care to All!

Entire nations are waking up and showing the way with empowered women as true leaders!

Spiritual practice now includes awakened political, economic and ecological practices.

Your awakened soul has tremendous power!
The power of Loving Attention is yours!
Use it to assist in the relief of suffering for ALL life here and now!

Emaho!

Many beaches,
One ocean.
Dive in—
Now!

About The Author

Lawrence Edwards grew up on Long Island, New York. His mystical experiences that first began as a young child led him to the formal study of meditation and psychology in undergraduate and graduate school. He studied with transpersonal psychologist, Dr. Kenneth Ring, at the University of Connecticut, and graduated magna cum laude in 1974. During this time, he practiced meditation and hatha yoga and began studying Tibetan Buddhism with Chogyam Trungpa Rinpoche. He continued practicing and studying in Buddhist and yogic traditions, which culminated in his training as a monk under the direct guidance of his Kundalini meditation master in India. He went on to earn a PhD from Temple University in 1986. His doctoral research was on delineating the types of psychological change and spiritual growth experienced through the long-term practice of a Kundalini-based yoga. Kundalini Shakti is the ancient yogic term for the innate universal power of Consciousness, transformation and revelation, which is the root of all forms of yoga. Later he received teachings and empowerments from H.H. the Dalai Lama, H.E. Tsewang Seetar Rinpoche, and Gelek Rinpoche.

In addition to practicing and teaching meditation for more than fifty years, Dr. Edwards is trained in Jungian depth psychology, biofeedback and neurofeedback, and is board certified in neuro-biofeedback (BCIA senior fellow). He has served on the board of directors and as president of the Northeast Regional Biofeedback Society. As a New York state licensed psychotherapist (LMHC), Dr. Edwards has been in private practice offering transpersonal psychotherapy for more than thirty years, and served on the faculty of New York Medical College since 1998.

Dr. Edwards is the founder and director of the Anam Cara Meditation Foundation, a 501(c)3 nonprofit educational organization that he started right after the 9/11 terrorist attacks, which had such a devastating impact on his suburban New York community and beyond. With the mission of Anam Cara (ancient Gaelic for "friend of the soul") to make the powerful transformative practices of meditation freely available to all, Dr. Edwards has offered free weekly meditation programs, in addition to retreats and courses for more than two decades. He continues to work with individuals and groups interested in deepening their meditation practices and spiritual development.

For more information, please visit:
www.anamcarameditation.org and www.thesoulsjourney.com

Other critically acclaimed writings by Lawrence Edwards include:
The Soul's Journey: Guidance From The Divine Within (2000)
Awakening Kundalini: The Path To Radical Freedom (2013)
Kali's Bazaar Penned by Kalidas (2012)

CPSIA information can be obtained
at www.ICGtesting.com
Printed in the USA
LVHW100706170622
721513LV00004B/375

9 780578 372280